The Making Mummies

by Rene Laplace

PEARSON

Scott
Foresman

Editorial Offices: Glenview, Illinois • Parsippany, New Jersey • New York, New York
Sales Offices: Needham, Massachusetts • Duluth, Georgia • Glenview, Illinois
Coppell, Texas • Sacramento, California • Mesa, Arizona

Why Make Mummies?

Like many people around the world, the people of ancient Egypt held special ceremonies when people died. They wanted to show respect to the person who died. The ancient Egyptians placed bodies in tombs. But they also wanted to preserve the bodies of their loved ones—the people they loved—before putting them in tombs. The process they used to preserve the bodies is called *mummification.* The preserved body is called a *mummy.*

The Egyptians preserved dead bodies by making them into mummies.

tombs: burial places built above the ground

preserve: to keep something from harm or change

mummy

In ancient Egypt making mummies was a very important job. Special priests learned how to do it. They began mummifying bodies about 4,600 years ago.

Before that time, the Egyptians had buried their dead in the desert sands. They noticed that the sand would dry out the bodies. The bodies buried in the desert sands were preserved. Maybe this is how the Egyptians got the idea to make mummies.

The Egyptians mummified bodies for almost 3,000 years. They used the basic steps explained in this book.

The jars for internal organs had lids shaped like the protecting gods.

Step 1: Internal Organs

Over the years, the Egyptians learned the best ways to preserve bodies. They knew it was most important to dry the body. They also knew that the internal organs of the body were the hardest parts to get dry. They solved this problem by removing the organs.

The priests removed the lungs, liver, intestines, and stomach. They placed each organ in its own jar.

The Egyptians believed that a different god protected each organ. They carved the lids of the jars to look like the four protecting gods.

---

internal organs: organs inside a body, such as a stomach

liver: an organ that helps the body digest food

intestines: the parts of the digestive system that extend below the stomach

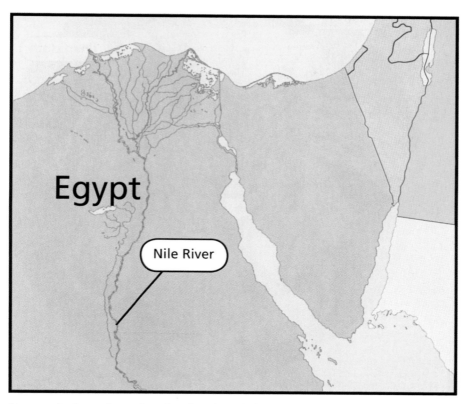

Natron is found on the riverbanks of the Nile River.

Step 2: Drying the Body

After removing the internal organs, the priests went on to the next step. They cleaned the inside and outside of the body. Then they used *natron* to dry the body. Natron is a combination of salt and a powder similar to baking soda.

Natron is abundant in Egypt. After the summer floods, there was a lot of natron near the banks of the Nile River. The Egyptians collected it and made it into a powder.

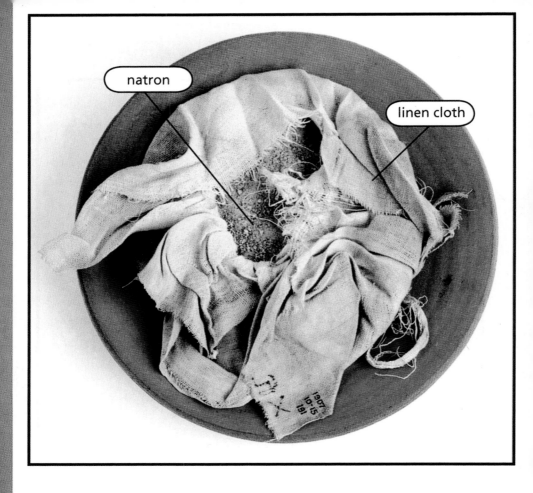

natron

linen cloth

The priests spread natron all over the outside of the body. They also filled cloth sacks with natron and put them inside the body. The priests waited about forty days for the body to dry. Then they washed the body and rubbed it with oil. The body was ready for the next step.

Step 3: Wrapping the Body

Next, Egyptian mummies were wrapped in narrow strips of linen cloth. The entire body was covered in many layers. The priests used hundreds of yards of linen for every mummy.

---

linen: cloth made from the flax plant

fingers

Each of this mummy's fingers was wrapped separately.

The bodies of powerful and wealthy people were wrapped with special care. For important people, the priests would wrap each finger, one by one. Then they wrapped the linen around the entire hand.

Sometimes they placed amulets among the linen strips. They thought the amulets would protect the dead person from harm.

The priests would also cover the linen with a sticky substance. When it dried, the sticky substance got hard and protected the mummy even more.

---

amulets: objects thought to be magic charms against evil or harm

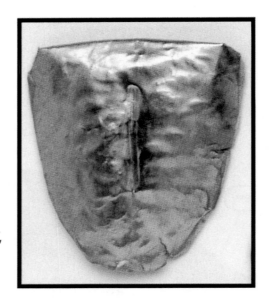

Important people got special treatment, such as this gold tongue covering.

Some of the mummies had fancy gold sandals to wear. Some had gold fingertips on their hands. Only the most powerful people, such as the pharaoh and his family, got this special treatment.

When the wrapping was finished, the priests tied linen strips all around to hold everything in place. The mummy was ready to be placed in a coffin.

Did You Know? The Pharaoh

The king of ancient Egypt was called a *pharaoh*. Pharaohs began ruling Egypt about 5,000 years ago. They had absolute power. Nobody could question what they did. Pharaohs had huge tombs called pyramids built to show the world what great kings they were. There were men and women pharaohs. The time of the pharaohs ended around 2,030 years ago.

---

pharaoh: royal leader, or king

coffin: box into which a dead person's body is put

Important people had many coffins, one inside another.

coffins

Coffins and Masks

Sometimes mummies were put into tombs after the wrapping was finished. But many mummies first were put into coffins. Some mummies were in a single coffin.

Important Egyptians would have as many as three coffins. The outer coffin was made of stone, and the other coffins were made of wood.

Some of the wooden coffins were covered with prayers written in hieroglyphics. The Egyptians also painted beautiful designs on the coffins. The head of the coffin often had a mask painted on it. Sometimes these masks were made of gold.

---

hieroglyphics: picture writing used by the Egyptians

Egyptians played the game *senet* on special tables or boards.

Helpful Items

Ancient Egyptians believed that their mummified loved ones would live for all eternity. They thought that their loved ones were going to a world very much like Egypt. So they put food, tools, clothing, furniture, and other household items into the tomb. They thought their loved ones would need these items in the next world.

Sometimes they even put games in the tomb with mummies. The Egyptians loved board games, especially a game called *senet*. One tomb had several full sets of senet games with their beautifully carved senet boards.

Shabtis were expected to act as servants in the next world.

Mummy's Little Helpers

Important people in Egypt had servants who helped them do everything during their lives. These people wanted the same kind of help in the next world. So their tombs contained little statues called *shabtis.*

Shabtis were supposed to be the servants in the next world. A shabti was usually just few inches high. Most were carved from wood or stone. Some were formed from clay.

Some shabtis held farming tools or baskets for collecting the harvest. Tombs sometimes contained hundreds of shabtis.

Non-human Mummies

Humans were not the only living things that were mummified. The Egyptians also preserved cats, monkeys, ducks, falcons, and crocodiles as mummies. Like humans, the animals were carefully wrapped in linen. Sometimes people kept animal mummies in their homes.

The Egyptians made millions of mummies. They stopped about 1,600 years ago after the Roman Empire took control of their land. But for 3,000 years, the Egyptians followed the art of making mummies.

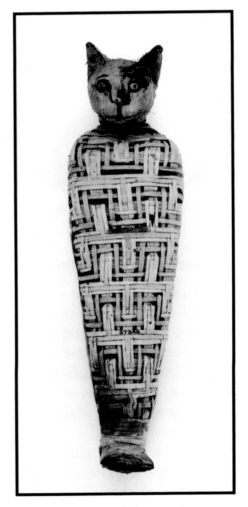

Cats were one of the most popular kinds of animals to mummify.